Prehistoric Cre

PTERANODON

By K.S. Rodriguez
Illustrated by Patrick O'Brien

STECK-VAUGHN
ELEMENTARY · SECONDARY · ADULT · LIBRARY

A Harcourt Company

www.steck-vaughn.com

To Jane Mason, great friend and editor

Produced by By George Productions, Inc.

Copyright © 2000, Steck-Vaughn Company

ISBN 0-7398-2147-4

Printed and bound in the United States of America
10 9 8 7 6 5 4 3 2 1 LB 03 02 01 00

Photo Acknowledgments:
Pages 6–7, 25: Department of Library Services, American Museum of Natural History; Page 17: The Field Museum; Page 21: Mark Burnett, Photo Researchers, Inc.

Contents

Pterosaurs Ruled the Skies   5

Pteranodon Talk   8

Unsolved Mysteries   16

Disappearing Act   21

Georges Cuvier—
Father of Paleontology   24

Make a Pteranodon   28

Glossary   30

Index   32

Pterosaurs Ruled the Skies

A giant creature flies through the sky. Its wings stretch out as wide as the length of a moving van. It flies down to the ocean and picks up a fish with its long beak. No, it is not a bird. It does not have feathers. Its wings are made of skin. No, it is not a bat, either. This creature is unlike any animal we know today. This creature is called a pterosaur. The best-known pterosaur was the Pteranodon.

Pteranodon was much larger than today's condor.

Pterosaurs lived hundreds of millions of years ago, long before people—and birds and bats—probably existed. It ruled the skies at the same time the dinosaurs ruled the earth. But it is not a dinosaur. *Pterosaur* means "winged lizard." Pterosaurs were flying reptiles.

Dinosaurs were reptiles that lived on land. Like dinosaurs, pterosaurs came in many shapes and sizes. Some pterosaurs were as small as sparrows. Some were much larger. A large pterosaur called Pteranodon is the best-known pterosaur of all.

7

Pteranodon Talk

Time Line ———————————

Mesozoic
(The era of the dinosaurs)

prosauropod	*Stegosaurus*	*Tyrannosaurus*
Triassic	**Jurassic**	**Cretaceous**
245 million to 208 million years ago	208 million to 145 million years ago	145 million to 65 million years ago

Pteranodon means "winged and toothless." This creature lived about 85 million to 65 million years ago, during the Cretaceous period.

Pteranodon's body was not much bigger than yours. But its wings spread out as wide as a truck is long. Pteranodon's body was covered with fur.

Cenozoic
(The era of mammals, including humans)

mammoth

human

Tertiary
65 million to
5 million
years ago

Quaternary
1.6 million
years ago
to today

Pteranodon's wings were as wide as the length of a large truck.

For many years scientists thought that Pteranodon was the largest pterosaur. But the discovery of another pterosaur, Quetzalcoatlus, changed that. The wings of Quetzalcoatlus stretched as wide as the length of two trucks— 40 feet (12 m)!

Like all pterosaurs, Pteranodon had light, hollow bones. This made flying easy, even though the creature was so big. Leathery wings hung down from its long fourth finger. Its other three fingers were short and had claws. It used them to climb trees and rocks.

Leathery wings stretched out from Pteranodon's fourth finger.

11

Pteranodon lived near oceans in what is now North America. Scientists think it made nests like birds. It probably made its nests on islands where predators like dinosaurs could not get to them.

Like birds and dinosaurs, Pteranodon laid eggs. Most experts think the creatures lived in family groups like birds. They may have raised their young as birds do, too. They may have cared for their babies and taught them how to fly.

Experts believe that Pteranodon probably cared for its young.

13

Like a pelican, Pteranodon glided over the water and picked up fish in its long beak. It could also pick up fish with the sharp point of its beak. Good eyes helped it spot fish from the sky.

Pteranodon ate many fish.

14

Pteranodon's long beak and crest

Pteranodon's head was almost as big as its body. Besides its long beak, it had a tall, thin crest on the top of its head. Scientists are not sure just what the crest was for. Some think it helped balance Pteranodon's heavy beak. Some think it helped it fly. It might have been used to help Pteranodon steer. We know many things about Pteranodon, but its crest is still a mystery. And there are many more mysteries.

Unsolved Mysteries

How did Pteranodon fly? How did it walk? These are two questions that still puzzle the experts.

Of course Pterosaurs lived long before humans. How do we know anything about them? Scientists called paleontologists study clues. The best clues are fossils.

Fossils are remains of life long ago. A fossil can be a bone or a footprint. It can be a mark of a creature left in a rock. Paleontologists look for fossils and study them to find out how Pteranodon looked and lived.

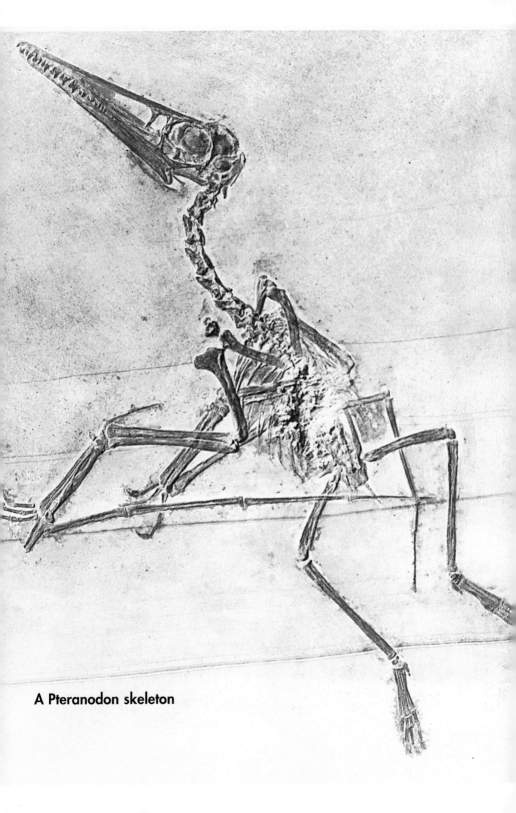

A Pteranodon skeleton

Scientists used to think that pterosaurs could only fly and glide. They did not think pterosaurs could flap their wings and fly like birds. Today experts believe that pterosaurs had strong flapping muscles. They look at Pteranodon's bones and think it was probably a very good flyer. It could travel long distances. But did it glide or flap more? Scientists are working to solve this mystery.

For years scientists have also wondered if Pteranodon walked on two legs like birds. Its hind legs seem very small. Could they have held up Pteranodon's whole body? Scientists used to think it must have used its hands to help it walk, as some bats do.

Some experts think pteranodon lived in family groups.

Experts think that Pteranodon was able to walk on its two legs. But it could not walk in a straight position.

Now more experts think Pteranodon could walk on two legs. But it probably did not stand up straight like birds. Instead it walked with its body tilted forward. Still, no one knows for sure which way Pteranodon walked.

These mysteries and more about Pteranodon keep scientists busy.

Disappearing Act

Though fossils do give paleontologists some answers, many mysteries remain about the flying lizards. The biggest mystery is why all the pterosaurs went away. Like dinosaurs, they disappeared, or became extinct, about 65 million years ago. Why? No one knows for sure.

Paleontologists digging for dinosaur clues

Pteranodon may have become extinct
because a change in Earth's air currents
made it difficult for the creature to fly.

22

Some scientists believe that whatever killed the dinosaurs killed the pterosaurs, too. Most think a huge rock from space, called a meteorite, hit Earth. Huge dust clouds were thrown into the air. They blocked out the sunlight. Without sunlight, plants would have died. Without any food, the plant eaters would have died. Soon the meat eaters that ate the plant eaters would have died, too.

Huge waves may have destroyed the animals' homes. It was not long before the dinosaurs and pterosaurs died.

Other scientists think maybe Earth's air currents changed. The change made it hard for pterosaurs to fly and feed. Still others think that early mammals ate too many of the pterosaurs' eggs.

Hopefully one day paleontologists will find more answers. Although pterosaurs have disappeared, we are still learning about them.

Georges Cuvier— Father of Paleontology

Georges Cuvier was born in France in 1769. He was one of the first people to study fossils. He named the first pterosaur in 1801. He was the first to say it was a winged reptile, not a bird or a bat.

Cuvier also introduced the idea of "extinction." To be extinct means that a kind of plant or animal no longer exists.

 24

Georges Cuvier
1769–1832

25

Cuvier was also one of the first people to say that Earth changed a lot over hundreds of millions of years. He realized that the planet was not the same as it was in the "Age of the Dinosaurs."

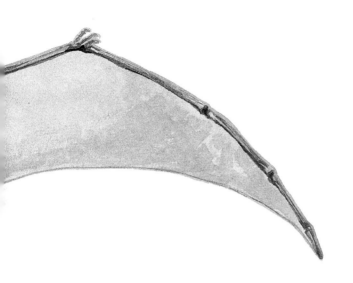

Cuvier worked most of his life as a professor
in the Museum of Natural History in Paris.
Because of his important work, France made
him a baron and a knight. Georges Cuvier died
in 1832, but his great ideas live on.

Make a Pteranodon

Note: This is a little tricky, so ask a grown-up to help.

Materials:

- piece of cardboard in the shape of a square—4 x 4 in. (10 x 10 cm)
- cardboard tube
- 1 manila folder
- scissors

1. Cut the piece of cardboard in half diagonally. On one of the triangles make a small cut about

1 in. (2.5 cm) from the base of the right angle. This triangle will be the head of the Pteranodon. You can use markers or crayons to draw in the eyes, mouth, and teeth.

2. Take the tube from a roll of paper towels. Along the side of the cardboard tube you should cut a straight line about 9 in. (23 cm) in length.

3. Cut off two inches of the manila folder so that it will be 9 in. (23 cm) long.

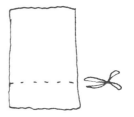

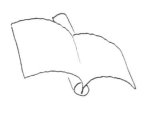

4. Stick the spine of the manila folder into the slit that you cut into the cardboard tube. The flaps of the manila folder form the Pteranodon's wings.

5. Attach the Pteranodon's head to the end of the cardboard tube that was not cut. Now when you move the Pteranodon up and down, its wings should flap.

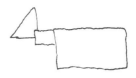

29

Glossary

crest (KREST) A growth on the head of an animal

Cretaceous period (kreh-TAY-shus) The time period from 145 million to 65 million years ago

dinosaurs (DIE-nuh-sores) Land-dwelling reptiles that lived from 245 million to 65 million years ago

extinct (ex-TINKT) No longer existing or living

fossil (FAH-sill) Remains of ancient life, such as a dinosaur bone, footprint, or imprint in a rock

mammals (MAM-ulls) Warm-blooded animals, usually with hair, that feed their young with milk

meteorite (MEE-tee-uh-rite) A rocky object from space that strikes the earth's surface. It can be a few inches or several miles wide.

paleontologist (pay-lee-on-TAH-luh-jist) A scientist who studies fossils

predator (PRED-uh-tur) A meat-eating animal that hunts and kills other animals

prehistoric (pree-his-TOR-ik) Time before written history

Pteranodon (tuh-RAN-uh-don) A large flying reptile with a bony crest on its head that lived in North America during the Cretaceous period

pterosaurs (TAIR-uh-sores) Group of ancient flying reptiles to which Pteranodon belonged

Quetzalcoatlus (ketz-ull-kuh-WATT-luss) The largest known pterosaur, with a wingspan of up to 40 feet (12 m)

reptile (REP-tile) A group of air-breathing animals that lay eggs and usually have scaly skin

Index

Age of the Dinosaurs 26
air currents 23

bat 5, 6, 19, 24
beak 5, 14, 15
bird 5, 6, 13, 19, 20, 24

crest 15
Cretaceous period 9
Cuvier, Georges 24, 26, 27

dinosaurs 6, 7, 13, 21, 23
dust cloud 23

Earth 23, 26
eggs 13, 23
extinct 21, 24

finger 11
fossils 16, 21, 24

mammals 23
meteorite 23
Museum of Natural History 27

nests 13
North America 13

paleontologists 16, 21, 23
Paris 27
pelican 14
predators 13
pterosaur 5, 6, 7, 10, 11, 16, 19,
  21, 23, 24

Quetzalcoatlus 10

reptiles 6, 24

waves 23
wings 5, 9, 10, 11, 19